KEYNOTES
FOR
COMPELLING
SELLERS

PHILIP LUND

To Margaret who gives me every inspiration

Published by Compelling Selling 2012
www.compellingselling.net

Book design and layout by Andy McColm
www.mccolmdesign.co.uk

ISBN 978-1-46792-674-4

CONFUCIUS
(551-479 BC)

Confucius taught the future business administrators of China's Emperors and ruling elite. As I read his sayings, I realized I was in fact reading a business book. Topics were recognizably modern business topics; and certain individuals in his text consistently spoke in particular ways and on particular themes. One sounds like a Finance Director, another like a Marketing Director and so on. It was a short step then to adapt the text to the modern business idiom yet still retain 98% of the original Confucian sayings in their English translation. The following excerpts are taken from Confucius & Co. – Thoughts of the Chairman.

Say it again Confucius!

If everyone dislikes it, it must be looked into. If everyone likes it, it must be looked into.

The Chief Accountant acted only after thinking thrice. Twice is quite enough.

Thoughts on Selling

"You will never sell anything unless you find your way to the decision maker."

 I'm always impressed how a well structured, balanced and thoughtful negotiation can change both the individual and the company.

 Saving costs is always worthwhile. Doubling turnover changes lifestyles. Top level negotiators make themselves.

 In the right circumstances he will also provide the 'sharp edge' of sales skills to take the product or service initially to market.

 Lots of amazings. Amazing too that Confucius' sayings then in 500BC can be read as a business text now.

 Funny how many people who offer products & services hate and deny they should be thought of as a sales person by anyone including themselves.

 Is sales really a battlefield? If it is, and the seller is doing the job properly, it is one of those nice battles where both sides win.

 How long should a negotiation take? Always Be Closing, the ABC of sales.

"The Sales Bible of Selling is *Compelling Selling*, more the 10 Commandments than Acts."

 We all need to know how to persuade to progress in our lives. Interestingly, it is never formally taught. Bit like biology – nice to know how it works.

 Most of us are taught by our Mums how to sell ourselves ie. a wack round the ear when we got it wrong.

 Makes me wonder if it was Mrs Carnegie who began the process to teach Dale how to win friends and influence people.

 Unlike most jobs, you know the value you are producing in selling because you have the orders in your pocket. Performance is rewarded.

Say it again Confucius!

If a manager does not give thought to problems which are still distant, he will be worried by them when they come nearer.

He who is fond of bravery but complains of poverty is going to create disorder.

Keynotes for Compelling Sellers
© 2012 Philip R. Lund

Say it again Confucius!

Let the other man do his job without interference.

A commander may be snatched from his army, but will cannot be taken from the humblest workman.

Keynotes for Compelling Sellers
© 2012 Philip R. Lund

"The trick at each stage of the sale is to make sure you have covered ALL the agreements. Summarise & confirm with the conditional close."

 Conditional close takes the customer thru to the next stage. "U said you wanted this, this & that. If I could give U these, would you....?"

 Do me a favour. When U give yr sales prospects, only use names who have said YES. Shows you have asked the last question. Even they fall off

 Exciting so many sales articles are using the words COMPELLING SELLING these days. Maybe we're becoming the 'hoover' of selling

 How? Why? When? Where? What? Who? What else do you need to know?

Why Selling?

"Most us use sales techniques heir mothers taught them, earning it's better to do and ay some things than others."

 Consequently people spend most of their time upsetting each other, an effect usually the exact opposite to one they are trying to achieve

 Whether selling a tangible product or a concept, the constant fact remains your objective is to meet your immediate customer's requirements

 Don't kid yourself you are the exception. Whether you are a famous company director or brain surgeon, the rules of persuasion are the same.

 You wouldn't have too much trouble setting an appointment with your spouse though selling the benefits of a course of action may be difficult.

 Selling has never been a matter of being a nice chap, persisting long enough, and relying on the other person to do what is best for himself.

Say it again Confucius!

To be Excellent engaged in administration is to be like the North Star. It remains in its one position as other stars dance arounnd it.

He whose language is unrestrained will have difficulty doing it all.

Keynotes for Compelling Sellers
© 2012 Philip R. Lund

Say it again Confucius!

A great Chairman does not accept a man for his words alone; he does not reject a suggestion because of the man alone.

A Great Chairman is no robot. First he sets a good example, then he invites others to follow it.

The Sales Framework

"The rules of persuasion are a sequence of defined steps to ensure every point relevant to the negotiation is adequately covered."

 If a persuader fully understands the framework of persuasion, he knows where he is at any one time and what he must do next.

 In selling, it is more effective to know than to feel; to know exactly what you want to achieve, how to set out for it, and what to do next.

 If you have a framework, you can compare and adjust for next time. Selling must always be the problem of the one that gets away.

 The framework first requires the salesman to identify the man he must sell too. No amount of talking will sell to the wrong man.

 Only when he has found his way to the decision maker can the seller open the interview

The Shape of a Sale

"Opening the interview then requires the seller to create the level of interest and the physical situation in which business can be discussed."

 Before introducing his offering, the seller must establish the customer's decision criteria 1, 2, 3,..The question is: Does he want it?

 To identify any pitfalls he must now preamble objections he knows from experience will give the customer the opportunity to avoid a decision.

 In selling benefits the seller shows the benefits his product offer match exactly the benefits or requirements the customer is seeking 1,2,3.

 The customer details exactly what he wants. The seller shows his benefits deliver these needs. Done properly the customer can only say YES.

 Keeping the customer sold requires constant reselling of current benefits. It is more difficult to win back one lost than find a new one.

Say it again Confucius!

The work people can be made to follow a System, but they cannot be made to understand it.

If those at the top are fond of rules, The work people are easy to direct. Instruction recognises no castes.

Say it again Confucius!

If one employs the competent as managers and instructs the less able, the workpeople will work hard.

Good management is of greater importance to workpeople than either fire or water. I have seen fire & water cause deaths but never good management.

Asking Questions

"The number one rule in human communication is: people prefer talking to listening. So learn to ask questions rather than make statements."

 Questions beginning HOW/WHY/WHEN/WHERE/WHAT/WHO? elicit qualitative answers to the topic you wish to discuss. YES/NO questions give control.

 I keep 6 honest serving men. They taught me all I knew. Their names are What and Why and When and How and Where and Who. KIPLING Just-So Stories

 Asking questions is the sine qua non of successful selling. Without questions you cannot find out what the customer wants to buy if anything.

 Questions allow you to set the subject for discussion, to retain the initiative and to continue along the lines of your questioning.

 Questions make you appear a pleasant and interesting person. If you have enough questions they will go on talking all day long.

 Questions let you to adapt your modes of expression to the person to whom you are talking & reply in the same terms. You don't have to act.

"As it is vital in the sale to obtain commitment, so it is important in any persuasion that seeks to modify behaviour whatever your occupation."

 To learn to persuade, if you don't know where to start, start here: learn to ask questions. There is only one way to do it. That is doing it

 There is no statement that can't be expressed as a question. Do this to restructure the way you communicate & become a better persuader.

 A top seller can carry a sale thru to the end making no statements, using only questions. Can you do the same? It changes the response to you.

We have ways of making you buy!

Say it again Confucius!

Am I a wise man? No! But if a lowly person asks me a question in complete ignorance I tell all I know from beginning to end.

Because of his lies, a man must be considered less than upright. Because of his uprightness, a man does not lie.

Keynotes for Compelling Sellers
© 2012 Philip R. Lund

Being fond of the company is better than merely knowing it. Taking delight in it is better than merely being fond of it.

If you have learned everything there is to know about the company in the morning, you may let yourself die that evening.

I am not concerned that a man does not know of me. I am concerned that I do not know of him.

Decisions are Emotional

"In persuasion the decision to act is emotional. Your logic may prove your loved one wrong to take an action but may well not change the action."

 Treating the sale within a framework allows the persuader to present a logical argument to deliver an emotional outcome without resistance.

 It does this thru questions to allow the respondent to define his own problem & then to list the criteria he feels must satisfy the solution.

 No-one likes making decisions. They take away another choice; and they tend to cost money. Remember your own resistance even to paying bills.

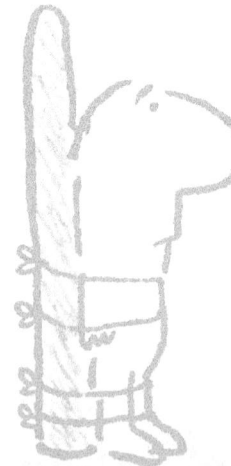

"The customer is expert at the problem, the salesman expert at the solution. This is how they come together to reach a successful decision."

 Then few people like decisions hanging over them. A seller is liked when he helps his client put a problem to bed, one less to think about.

 A customer wants a decision, not a choice. He wants to be put thru the decision process expertly. That is the salesman's role, expert advisor.

 Whatever the form of persuasion, no decision is ever made unless it is explicitly demanded and given. 'Are you happy to proceed?' ' YES'

 If you leave without actually asking for the decision, the chances are your respondent has emotionally avoided making one. HAS HE SAID YES YET?

Say it again Confucius!

I once went all day without food & all night without sleep to help me think. I found no advantage in it; its best to study.

Just as artisans inhabit the market place to ply their trades, so a great manager studies to improve his skills.

Keynotes for Compelling Sellers
© 2012 Philip R. Lund

Say it again Confucius!

As a clever remark can ruin another's Excellence so, if there is the slightest impatience, a grand scheme can be ruined.

As you serve your Chief Executive, give precedence to his interest. Think of your reward last.

Study as if you were to never master it; as if in fear of losing it.

What makes a Seller?

"Great salesmen are self-made developing skills of intelligence & perception to understand the customer's real problem, self motivation..."

...& enthusiasm to generate new ideas resilience to capitalise on the good times, self criticism to review costantly his own performance.

...discipline most importantly to work t plan, control what he does & what he says, to control the customer thru the decision path; & finally.

...ambition to succeed & integrity: 'like virginity you can only lose it once. Unlike virginity there is never a better time to lose it' (anon).

Plan it!

"Selling is a hard professional business. The prize and rewards go to the seller with a hard professional attitude."

 Learn by calling existing customers to stay in touch with their thinking, their problems and the way they see your product's value.

 The optimum presentation has the fewest words and actions. Adding to these only places the salesman at additional risk of losing the order.

 A top salesman must constantly monitor own performance. Even with the order won, some words & attitudes could have been used & taken better.

 Over familiarity can influence a salesman's judgement of what is important. What is unimportant to him can be very relevant to the customer.

 A salesman should appear an interesting & competent businessman. First impressions are lasting impressions.

 A salesman must appear at least as good as the person to whom he is selling. Knowledge and ability are always respected.

Say it again Confucius!

He who engages solely in self-interested actions will make himself many enemies.

The two tea ladies were never mindful of wrongs done to them; hence they had few enemies.

There is a saying: 'Speak about your superiors as though they were actually present in person.'

Clever talk and a domineering manner have little to do with being a good manager.

Keynotes for Compelling Sellers
© 2012 Philip R. Lund

Say it again Confucius!

When you see a man of high calibre, give thought to attaining his stature. When you see one who is not, conduct a self-examination.

Put loyalty & reliability first. Have no friends inferior to yourself. If you have faults, don't fear self-improvement.

Wealth and honours are what men desire; but, if they come undeserved, don't keep them.

"There is no advantage in raising yourself above or reducing yourself below your respondent. The game you play convincingly is your own game."

In selling, the decision to sign is emotional even when the reasons to sign are logical. Salesmen who sell are salesmen who can motivate.

Producing & selling products are 2 problems. The sales problem must be absorbed else the market lives with the mouse than find the mousetrap

The difference in output between an ordinary & good seller is +100%, & a brilliant seller + another 100%. How good are you? It's your choice.

Know your 'Product'

"Customers buy a 'product' for the benefit and solutions it will bring them.. Cars maybe the exception."

 The seller must know what his product is so he can know what it does. Only then can he sell the benefits to the customer.

 The seller must know his product benefits for each type of customer to bring forward the 2 or 3 benefits critical to any specific activity.

 Unless it's a technical product, too much technical detail beyond answering simple questions is selling to the wrong person or the wrong way.

 What is important is your product/service is capable of doing what you say it can. A short explicit statement of how should be sufficient.

 Too much technical detail emphasises what it is rather than its benefits. It may bring applause but not sales: exception scientific products.

 The seller must know how users use his product so he knows the questions he needs to ask similar companies. They're also good 3rd party refs.

Say it again Confucius!

Poverty and low estate are what men dislike; but, if they come undeserved, don't flee them.

Is it not true that some shoots do not survive while others survive but produce no grain?

It is enough that one's words express fully one's thought.

As night is not as black as it is painted, so a Chairman shuns low company for fear the evils of the world will be imputed to him.

Keynotes for Compelling Sellers
© 2012 Philip R. Lund

Managing
Successful Selling

"A seller must be encouraged continually. He works on his own and lives with problems. He does not call the office to hear what he has not done."

 The seller must have what he needs to succeed. He must not think he is fighting for the company in the field & against it in the office.

 The seller must know about his competitor what he knows about his products. He must know the answer to the question before it is asked.

 A seller is a team player & know how he stands in relation to his colleagues with meetings & social interaction. Success must be rewarded.

 The seller must know why customers prefer competitive products even if it means calling to find out. Similarly he must know their services.

 The seller becomes convinced with his product's benefits thru the customers' response to them. It is a bad product that offers nothing.

 If the seller loses faith he cannot sell. If his product offers no significant benefits to the competitor's, then it's time to change sides!

Being Professional

"Sellers, don't moan every time things go wrong with product or delivery. Things do go wrong. Use it to show the strength of your response."

 Remember all products are different even if the difference is the seller selling. So be different & be better. U are the person 2 deal with.

 When a customer buys, his opinion of you is important. He knows sooner or later he will have problems which he will want you to sort out.

 Remember. You fight for your company in the field and for your custopmer with the company. Be sure he wants & knows how to get hold of you.

 Be creative. When you have an idea, try to 'explode' it. Discover what is good about it and how it is best used. Then you will develop it.

 When a customer buys, his opinion of you is important. He knows sooner or later he will have problems which he will want you to sort out.

Say it again Confucius!

A man who has rendered himself correct will have no trouble managing. If he can't render himself correct how can he correct others.

He who is unflinching, bold, simple, natural and unhurried approximates a good manager.

This is certainly the limit. I have yet to meet a man who, on observing his own faults, blamed himself.

Keynotes for Compelling Sellers
© 2012 Philip R. Lund

Planning to Sell

"A seller's sales plan is the company plan divided by the number of salesmen divided by 52 weeks in the year or 13 periods of 4 weeks."

 If a seller doesn't have a sales plan he doesn't know what he is doing. If his manager doesn't know the plan, he can give no guidance.

 To plan well, a seller must know the time cycle & type of calls for each category of customer & the number of calls to convert a new order.

 The sales plan is the agreement reached between the seller and his manager. It should detail what each requires of the other in support.

 Too low sales targets encourage laziness, too high hopelessness. A seller needs a target he can reach and surpass with good effort & reward.

 The seller must decide whether to sell big orders or more small orders. His incentive scheme will encourage him to do it the simplest way.

 If you have a monthly sales target, achieve it monthly. Don't kid yourself you can take the orders next month. You won't. You'll fall behind.

Planning Rules

"A new customer is one the company has not done business with before. New business comes from new customers. New customers mean real growth."

 The seller must judge value potential of both new & existing customers. Bigger profitable orders now are better than smaller orders later.

 No seller needs feel he will take fewer orders than others. The weaker his conversion rate, the more calls he needs to make to take orders.

 A good seller gets out of bed knowing exactly what he will do. He has planned ahead. 08.30-17.30 he can take the risk of taking orders.

 08.30-17.30 is prime selling time, that is customer face-to-face meeting time. Complainers can be let to 17.00 when they're too tired to talk.

 Between 17.00 & 09.00 the seller can do things that do not require the customer to be there- emails, reports, research & a good night's sleep.

 Truth to tell, and unhappily for most sellers, mind produces more business than strength. Think it out properly; and make JFDI your motto.

Say it again Confucius!

Shall I tell you what knowledge is? It is to know both what one knows and what one does not know.

It is indeed harmful to come under the sway of utterly new and strange doctrines.

Let the sole worry of your superiors be that you might become ill.

Keynotes for Compelling Sellers
© 2012 Philip R. Lund

Say it again Confucius!

The ages of the managers over you must always be known, both as a source of joy and as a source of dread.

I can do absolutely nothing for a man who will not bring me his problems.

Why does no-one follow this doctrine of mine just as naturally as they leave my office by the door?

"The scarcity in selling is time. Spend selling time selling. The customer to see now is the customer who will give you his order now."

 The seller is running a small business or his territory. He should treat his territory that way and be treated that way.

 The seller must not become manager dependant. If he cannot make decisions on his own, his customers never will. Managers supply back-up only.

 If the seller knows how long to take an order, he knows when to begin. Selling to government or utilities, you must match their budget dates.

 Sellers should plan by numbers – # value sales, # face to face contacts, # presentations/quotes, # new contacts, # existing customer contact.

The Key Sales Parameters

"The key sales control is the number of hot prospects you need to match your order take-off. All other calls replace this wastage"

 The key definition: a hot prospect is a new or existing customer who says YES he will place his NEW order subject to ie Board agreement.

 Each hot prospect will give the seller 65% chance of realisation. The seller has actually asked and the customer has said YES.

 Seller - if you reach your sales target by Wednesday, don't start preparing for next week's orders. Take them this week. That makes money.

 The seller runs a small business. He presents to his markets, sells to it, arranges delivery, creates new end uses & profits from the sales.

 The only way a small business can be run is through planning – by geographical coverage, category of customer and speed & value of ordering.

 From his call patterns, the seller needs a shrewd idea of the number of customers needed in each stage of negotiation for his order pipeline.

Say it again Confucius!

The mere assumption of burdens, the mere allowing of elders to be first to eat or sleep does not constitute loyalty.

Asked if it is better to be on good terms with the accountant, he replied: 'Whoever offends the Chairman has no court of appeal'.

Look at the means which a man employs, consider his motives, observe his pleasures. A man cannot conceal himself.

Keynotes for Compelling Sellers © 2012 Philip R. Lund

Selecting the Startpoint

"Worry about orders you will take this year & let orders you will take next year look after themselves. The company survives on orders now."

 You are likely to find new customers where you have existing customers – a market for complimentary products & where you will find competitors.

 For starters the seller needs to define the nature of exisiting customers to identify businesses with similar same ordering potential.

 Take care the spread of exisiting customers does not describe only the efforts of the previous seller. Most prospects he leaves will be dead.

 The previous seller will have done everything to close out his prospects. His failure is in the notes he leaves. Probably the wrong contact.

 Sales areas have an interesting characteristic. The better they are worked the better they work next time. Use a fresh approach to the unsold.

Keynotes for Compelling Sellers
© 2012 Philip R. Lund

"Spend more sales time in those areas that produce bigger, better orders understanding competitors will arrive in areas you neglect."

 Start selling to slow big future orders now. Know why similar business are not using similar products in a similar way for low hanging fruit.

 Companies in a similar business or using products in a similar way constitute similar markets even though the words you use may be different.

 A good seller balances his workload between long, medium and short term prospect top fill his order pipeline at an ever increasing rate.

 Long term prospects often have multi-order potential, medium require decisions on market segments & short is where competition strikes first.

Say it again Confucius!

Excellence does not remain alone. It is sure to attract neighbours.

Fate begat Excellence in me. How can my adversaries harm me?

To engage in gossip is to cast aside Excellence.

Continuous readaptation to suit the whims of others undermines Excellence.

I have yet to meet a manager as fond of Excellence as he is of outward appearances.

Keynotes for Compelling Sellers
© 2012 Philip R. Lund

Say it again Confucius!

An Excellent man will always have something to say; but those who do not speak are not necessarily Excellent men.

A good manager will be courageous; but all the courageous are not necessarily good managers.

On management 'Require of others only what you have first taught them'. Asked for further guidance 'Never grow weary'.

4 Planning Rules

"Rule 1 – Increase effective selling time available to you by keeping selling time to selling, not sitting in your car or planning."

 Planning Rule 2 – Increase the number of effective calls you make to decision makers with ordering potential.

 Planning Rule 3 – Reduce the number of calls you make to any one customer to take his order and so make more selling time available.

 Planning Rule 4 – Improve your conversion rate of New prospective customer to New orders by selling to quick, big, New decision makers first.

The Framework of the Sale

"The sale has 3 stages: INTEREST to discuss the problem, DESIRE to accept your solution; and CLOSE when he finalises his decision."

 INTEREST in the sale, when the customer talks about himself and his issues, always comes first. Your product is barely mentioned.

 DESIRE is created by benefit selling as the seller shows how his product provides solutions in words the customer used to describe his issue.

 The final CLOSE is the question the seller uses to ask the the customer to make his decision as in 'Are you now happy to go ahead'?

Say it again Confucius!

On the day he made one of his executives redundant, the Chairman did not sing.

The executives of old never exaggerated for fear that they themselves would not live up to their lofty sentiments.

When strict with oneself one rarely fails.

A manager can make a system great. It is not the system that makes the manager great.

Say it again Confucius!

My predecessor was ashamed of clever talk, a domineering manner and overdeference. I'm ashamed of them too.

He was ashamed to act in a friendly manner towards a man while inwardly angry with him. So am I.

Extravagence leads to disobedience, parsimony to miserliness. Of the two I prefer miserliness.

Those who know about Excellence are indeed few.

Keynotes for Compelling Sellers
© 2012 Philip R. Lund

Set Sales Objectives

"It is unlikely a seller will lose a sale by trying to close it too often. He will certainly lose it if he does not close."

 As a point of honour, a seller should try to close at least once every meeting, however hopeless it looks. The customer might just say YES.

 Every sale has a primary objective to take the order. Each contact or call has a secondary objective to close ie to set the appointment.

 Secondary objectives are steps along the way to take the order. Both objectives follow the same path INTEREST, DESIRE, CLOSE. No exceptions.

 Whether phoning, calling, emailing, presenting you must hit the customer's interest first time. If you fail, he will hit the delete button.

 Immediate impact is essential. You must know what you will say before you say it. Stutter or stumble, you will lose his interest & business.

 One way is to be interesting yourself. Sound as though you are worth hearing. Work out a style. Be enthusiastic. No one else is going to be.

Getting the Sale Underway

"If the seller phrases the right question, he will draw an interested answer. Maybe from something you know or see entering his office."

 Another way is to make a statement that will cause the customer to ask a question. Even the hardest man will wait and listen to the answer.

 Once the seller has caught the customer's attention, he must convert it into interest in discussing the problem. Now the sale is underway.

 Benefit selling creates desire for the product as the customer thinks he has solved a problem. He begins to want what it will do for him.

 When the customer has all the LOGICAL evidence that he has a solution to his problem he can make an EMOTIONAL commitment to a final decision.

 The customer becomes involved in his own decision. It becomes important for him to make a decision. He becomes more than logically involved.

Say it again Confucius!

To note things in silence, to retain curiosity despite study, never to weary teaching others: no-one surpases me in these things.

I should like to bring security to the aged, to be loyal to my friends, to be affectionate with the young.

Stir emotions with job descriptions. Assign proper roles. Provide a pleasing atmosphere with music if necessary.

Keynotes for Compelling Sellers
© 2012 Philip R. Lund

Say it again Confucius!

My son could be called loyal, for no-one speaks of him any differently from his parents and brothers.

A small minded man-ager always glosses over his own faults.

He who is conscious of his lacks and every month checks he is neglecting none of his abilities - that man is fond of learning.

Keynotes for Compelling Sellers
© 2012 Philip R. Lund

"If the right pressure is applied in the right way to the emotional side of a man's nature, he will buy. The sale will move on to the CLOSE."

 The seller must do everything to increase the emotional content of the sale without breaking continuity – visual or word pictures, proposals.

 At this point of the sale, the seller must retain tight control. The customer must be moved relentlessly to the point when he will sign the order.

 The customer will seek to flee the sense of mounting pressure. The seller must remove any chance for escape. All points covered, he must close.

 The seller must CLOSE firmly. If the job has been properly done the only thing left for ther customer to say to the invitation to buy is YES.

Sales Controls

"New business comes from new or existing customers where new business is discussed for the first time. Growth comes from new business"

 Repeat orders from existing customers should already be yours if you have treated them properly & shown interest as they use your products.

 As the sales cycle proceeds, new contacts become new prospects, then new GOOD prospects, then new HOT prospects, then new orders.

 If the seller converts 1 in 3 prospects into an order & knows how many calls to take that order, then he has the basis for a sales plan.

 If you exhaust 3 hot prospects to take 1 order then you have to create 3 new hot prospects from new calls and good prospects to replace them.

 The harder U sell the heavier the whip U make to beat your own back ie more calls made, more follow-up calls to make. The only way is to plan.

 The key is to increase the sales success rate & reduce the selling time. If you have a problem, copy a successful colleague who has the trick.

Say it again Confucius!

Let mourning stop after full expression of our grief.

Three facets of a great manager. From a distance he seems stern, close range he is pleasant; & his words clear cut.

Although he is a friend of mine and capable of many difficult things, he is not yet a great manager.

Keynotes for Compelling Sellers
© 2012 Philip R. Lund

Say it again Confucius!

If there is spare time holding office, let it be given to study. If there is spare time studying, let it be given to holding office.

Although he makes a fine impression, it is hard to achieve good management at his side.

Management's Role

"The sales manager is part of th sales team. His task is to help th seller achieve his corelated targe not sit in judgement over him."

 The seller should share with his manager what he needs to meet his sales targets. Market research is better done by market researchers.

 A seller's job is to produce orders. Giv him other tasks and he will be off doin them with the good excuse why he ha failed to deliver.

 A seller can only be effectively motivated with financial incentives to optimise time use,...achieving targets & dealing with customers.

 If the sales manager thinks he takes orders and deals with customers, he throws away any hope the seller will work effectively on his own.

 7 sellers in a team, properly managed & motivated, sell more than a sales manager who thinks he can ride in roughshod to pick off big orders.

 Motivating sellers is a sales task. How? Why? When? Where? What? Who? see opinions & allow managers' views to b part of the sellers' thinking.

The Sales Control Ratio

"The key sales control ratios are – Orders: hot prospects, new calls: total calls & key calls: total calls. Key calls are must do calls like demos"

Say it again Confucius!

Even if a manager has never done a thing whole heartedly, he must do so on the death of a colleague.

 For sales management, numbers are more important than promises. Hot prospects have already said YES and New calls are new business calls.

 Sales come from hot prospects. Hot prospects are decision makers who have said YES but must await, say, Board decision delaying signature.

 If you target one sale a week, exhausting 3 hot prospects to do it, the sales task is to replace the 3 hot prospects from good prospects.

 If 5 good prospects replace 3 HOT Ps & GPs come from new & existing customers @ a 2:1 conversion rate, the sales task is 10 calls + closing.

 # quotations is not good as a measure of future success. Quotes confirm decisions. Asking 4 quotes is a good way to be rid of a bad seller.

The Sales Control Docs

"Sales control docs are Revenue Pipeline Schedule, Client Contact Report, Daily Call Sheet, Customer Records, Forward Plans & Expense Form."

 Revenue Schedules shows by month/value booked revenue, hot prospects @65% & Good Prospects @ 35% by new & exist clients. HPs list date of order.

 Client Contact Report shows daily by number only, new, follow-up, user & technical calls, demos/presents made, # & value of quotes & orders.

 Daily Call sheet for new sellers for a short time shows by client call purpose and call outcome and value to ensure clear sales objectives.

 Forward plans are a diary to ensure the seller is planning ahead by geography & product. Expense forms check spend & time in front of client

Choose Your Markets

"Markets that turn profitable are often very different from the innovator's thinking. How different customers use it makes different markets."

 Only good selling challenges traditional operating methods & establishes new markets for new products in new areas as sellers define need.

 The wider the range of product use the more likely it is to succeed, the smaller the range the more important customer commitment at design.

 Having found the markets finding the companies to sell is simple. Key now is to find linkages thru knowledge & contacts to warm your approach.

 Having chosen you, customers are only too happy to share with you friends in business who could use your products. Make sure you ask them.

 Always check for the decision maker. Companies differ in the responsibility they give employees so be sure you're selling to the right man.

 The first customer to sell to is the one who will place his order now. Sell to him or your competitors will.

Say it again Confucius!

A Great Chairman does not show blind persistence in his practice of uprightness.

A Great Chairman's concern is that he might die without a good name.

Keynotes for Compelling Sellers
© 2012 Philip R. Lund

Using Sales Time

"Sales brain complements sales brawn. Which clients need it now, just moved, have new products, changed methods, buy easily. Hit them first."

 Time is the expensive scarcity in selling. Pattern your calls to get maximum response per unit of selling time. Use selling time to sell.

 You SELL by face to face contact. You PROGRESS sales on the phone. Write quotations, emails, reports and presentations outside selling time.

 Decide which call path is quickest to the order. Should I cold call first or telephone for an appointment or set up a presentation/demo.

 And remember this. Probabilities multiply. If there are 3 steps in a sale each with a 70% chance, the probability of a sale is c35% not c70%.

Sell to Decision Makers

"The man to see is the man who makes the decision. He can authorise the placing of the order. How to get to him is the basic selling problem."

 A seller must be able to identify & get in front of his decision maker. However good at presentation, he will fail for this one reason.

 No amount of selling will sell to the wrong man. You can talk your heart & soul away but, if he is not the right man, you will not sell.

 You are selling to the wrong man if he goes elsewhere for the decision. The other man is the right man for you. Needs be, see both together.

 Although the sales argument is logical, the decision to make a decision is emotional. You cannot transmit this message thru a 3rd party.

 If you find you are selling to the wrong man, it is usually better to break off diplomatically and rearrange with the right man or with both.

 The buyer isn't usually the right man unless you sell to retail. The buyer usually deals with the mechanics of buying.

Say it again Confucius!

The Great Chairman uses books to bring together friends; and through friendships he bolsters good management.

A Great Chairman calculates in terms of grand strategy, not in terms of earning a living!

Keynotes for Compelling Sellers
© 2012 Philip R. Lund

Say it again Confucius!

A Great Chairman must be mindful to see when he looks, to hear when he listens and to be loyal in speech.

The Great Chairman must also be mindful to have a facial expression of gentleness, an attitude of humility and to inquire when in doubt.

"The rule of thumb is to go high. You can always go down in an organisation but almost never g up. Titles can be misleading too.

 If buying your product involves a change in company policy in some way, then the Director of the business unit is your decision maker.

 If your case is strong & your decision maker will not see you, you have the right to go to his MD. You cannot lose an order that you have not got.

 Finding the right decision maker is asking the right questions: 'He does this?' 'She does this?' Who do they both report to?

 Don't tell your story to people on the way to the decision maker. Information that cannot be used for you will be used against you.

 Remember you are employed at the same level as the person you will talk to, not the person questioning you. This helps maintain control.

 Don't be persuaded to say why you want to talk to the decision maker. That's your concern, not theirs. Their job is to put you through.

 Speak with authority. Sound in charge important & they will not risk questions Asked why you want to speak to him, reply with a question

Selling is an Emotional Event

"Sellers who sell have the ability to overcome the reluctance to buy with the emotional appeal that the decision is right & worth taking."

 Customers are reluctant to make decisions because they cost money & preclude an alternative decision, if only to do NOTHING.

 Customers buy to satisfy primary personality needs that influence actions & and secondary business needs to have a product that performs.

 In selling stressing more money is not good motivation. People think 'money is bad but what it buys is OK'. What money does is good.

 Customers have 6 primary psychological needs including success (power, status, money as applause), esteem (being loved, attractive, manly).

 ...need for permanence (physical health, reputation, reputation, immortality) & possession (ownership of success, things worth having) &....

 ..need for comfort (ability to relax, what money will buy, avoid problems) & security (freedom from pain, worry, fear, money in continuity).

Say it again Confucius!

A Great Chairman must have an attitude of humility, to think of difficulties when angry, to think of justice when he seeks advantage.

A Great Chairman can be entrusted with a child's education and the rule of a state. At crisis times he remains unshaken.

Say it again Confucius!

A Great Chairman studies widely for refinement but adheres to the code of law and thus commits no transgressions.

A Great Chairman teaches four things: literature, conduct, loyalty and reliability.

"Each person is made up from a combination of primary motivators & a view of himself (ego ideal). The seller must recognise & appeal to them."

 The seller discovers these motivators seeing how his customer dresses, the way he lives, his car, his office, the life values he attributes.

 Words like success/esteem/permanence/possession/comfort/ security all become important as the seller describes benefits his product delivers.

 The customer has a primary requirement for justice and good treatment. The seller must be honest on price & product qualities or he is dead.

 Sales gains through deceit are short lived. Repeat orders and recommendations are the name of the selling game. Integrity is paramount.

Keynotes for Compelling Sellers
© 2012 Philip R. Lund

Set Clear Call Objectives

"Sales objectives fall into 2 categories: call objectives or agreements along the negotiation & planning objectives or category of calls made."

 A seller's approach is his primary objective to take the customer order NOW. He must do every thing necessary & nothing unnecessary to do it.

 The seller must close the order or he must close his next objectives ie place order next week, or subject to quote, or agree to presentation.

 The sales objective is closed when the seller asks for decision & the customer says YES. He would 'love to do it' is not commitment. YES is.

 Seller- the customer saw you because he has a problem in your area. Leaving without a decision, he still has the problem & has wasted time.

 Without seeking a decision, the customer cannot clarify his requirements. Without expression of objections how can he know if they are valid.

 Sellers are solution experts but the customer is expert on the problem. Your solution will innovate on the requirements so develop your case.

Say it again Confucius!

Our country without a recognised leader is still preferable to foreign countries for all their leaders.

If I mention one corner of a subject and an executive does not deduce therefrom the other three, I drop him..

Keynotes for Compelling Sellers
© 2012 Philip R. Lund

Call Categories

"There are 9 call categories. The telehone call sets the meeting o progresses the decision. Critical objections must be handled face-to-face."

 Face-to-face NEW CALLS introduce new concepts driven by your product. FOLLOW-UP CALLS take the order or restress mutual business benefits.

 EMAILS confirm product benefits & dates & times of meetings. QUOTA-TIONS should only confirm agreements on price & spec already reached.

 USER CALLS confirm stocking, fight off competition & take repeat orders, TECHNICAL CALLS ensure everyone is happy & demos confirm the magic.

 Set your objective precall. Take care customer enthusiasm does not persuade you to vary it & lose call structure & control. Can be fatal.

 In doubt? Sales objective rule is to aim high & settle for lesser: close for order & settle for demo, close for 2 orders & settle for one.

 Changing products midstream to solve same problem is disasterous. Make sure you fully understand the issue & position the correct product.

"Customer has the right to your good faith in negotiation. In doubt on size of fit? Aim high, sell hard, let him decide. Big can be better."

 Establish the right call objective. Approach every sale as though it is the most difficult you will have to make. That means don't take risks.

Say it again Confucius!

How do we evaluate a man who, while maintaining Excellence, does not further its influence?

How do we evaluate a man who, having put his faith in the System, is not sincere?

Say it again Confucius!

I do not instruct the uninterested; I do not help those who fail to try.

Who fails to recognise Fate can never become a Great Chairman. Who fails to follow laws can never play his proper role.

Cold Calling

"With modern office security cold calling can be difficult; but don't drive past an opportunity without calling to get contact name & number."

 Cold calling also gives you familiarity with the site important when you call; and a chat with someone in the yard can pull out usful themes.

 "A just passing by & thought I would pop in to see you" call can be useful with a customer too busy to get down to putting pen to paper.

 Use call cards sparingly if at all on a cold call. If he knows you will call, you give him the chance to decide not to see you, no word spoken.

Setting the Appointment

"The more information you give away on the way to the decision maker the less chance you have reaching him. You give them discretion & control."

 Seller – Staff want to exercise decision & control over you. Information that can't be used for you will be used against you. True of life too.

 Getting through to the appointment is largely a control problem, handled as any selling situation. You ask questions that require answers.

 Well chosen words & confidence set appointments. You are on the same level & have the right to an interview. Speak to God, not the saved.

 Closing to pass receptionist or secretary, to talk to decision maker, to set appointment is about strong, positive & focus on objective.

 Control technique to pass receptionist is to use question answer question
"Please put me thru to Joe X"
"Who is speaking"
"Lund. Is he in?"

Say it again Confucius!

Who does not know the value of words will never come to understand his fellow men.

While you have superiors, do not wander far. Let your sojourning only be in places you have already specified.

Say it again Confucius!

If a company is follow-ing a System, you may speak and act boldly. If it is not, let your acts be bold but your speach accomodating.

"Why do you want to meet him?" "It is really rather complicated. Will Tuesday at 10am suit him. Or will Wednesday 10.30 be better?"

 "Who do you represent?" "Trellis Ptnrs. Is he in?" "When is he free?" "Is next week more suitable?" "Isn't it a beautiful day?"

 Remember. Don't be rude. She's a better friend than an enemy. She also has to cope with other cretinous calls all day. So be interesting.

 If the decision maker is not in, call back another day. Don't be put off.. Seeing the wrong person is a sure way to fail, to lose the sale.

 Telephones are good to set appoint-ments, keep in touch, extend invita-tions, seek information, confirm meet--ings BUT NOT TO CLOSE THE SALE.

 Closing the sale is a face-to-face event because you could hit objections. Handling objections you must be there where the order is signed.

Telephoning

"Telephones cover ground quickly & give you control to open the conversation. But the receiver can be replaced just as easily. No hesitation!"

 First impressions are important. On the phone first bad impressions are fatal. Know what you are going to say & make sure it's interesting.

 Telephones are for setting appointments, not letters or emails. If you can't say what you have to say on the phone you should not be selling.

 Once you have set the meeting on the phone, confirm it with thanks & say goodbye. If you stay on the phone you can only lose the appointment.

 If the customer says phone back later, set meeting provisionally to be confirmed. Never leave recall numbers. You must retain the initiative.

 If the customer accepts meeting but wants more information, say it's better kept for the meeting. Otherwise he may decide he knows enough.

 You must pass the telephonist. Insist she puts you through. "Who is speaking?" "Lund. Please put me through". Strong. Intelligent, not rude.

Say it again Confucius!

The joke the Chairman tells in the Boardroom expresses joy but is not lewd; it expresses grief but not laceration.

Keynotes for Compelling Sellers
© 2012 Philip R. Lund

Say it again Confucius!

When eating beside a man who was not feeling well, the Chairman never ate his fill.

A Great Chairman is completely at ease; a small minded Chairman always on edge.

Keynotes for Compelling Sellers
© 2012 Philip R. Lund

"Don't get sidetracked into talking to the telephonist. She can be your friend second time round. Make sure there is a second time."

 If you fail to get through, don't be persuaded to send on information. You'll be wasting your time and killing off a prospect. Call later.

 The telephone is an important tool if you have agreed a decision timetable but never call unless you can ask or offer something interesting.

 Call your prospect the day after the meeting or quotation to see if he has any queries, to confirm agreements & progress of the negotiation.

 With the prospect on the phone first call, yours must be the one to sound different. Make the bait interesting and he will snap at it.

 First call on the phone, get the prospect asking questions: a fine rule in selling. Once he asks, he won't stop you telling him the answers.

 One way to interest is to sound interesting. Smile while you are phoning. Have references to hand of people & things he knows to make links.

 Remember the purpose of the first phone call is to set a meeting. If you must demo your product, why not a demo? That achieved, time to go.

'Key to setting the meeting
s the alternative close. "Is
Monday at 10.00 suitable or
Wednesday 11.15? Let's decide
on the date, not the WHY."

 If he asks a question, make a statement & another question close. It keeps the pressure on & the call short. If you get silence, stay silent.

 Keep price discussions until the end of the sale when you can show value. If pushed you need to know what he wants before you say how much.

 In selling, price = value. If your product has high value to your customer, your price can be cheap; low value and it is always expensive.

 The seller must get through to the end of the sale before customer can understand the real value in his decision & whether the price is good.

 If you do not close, you will not sell. If you do not close the appointment on the phone, you will never get to the next stage in the sale

Say it again Confucius!

From his study of business a Great Chairman comes to love his colleagues, a small minded chairman becomes distainful.

Keynotes for Compelling Sellers
© 2012 Philip R. Lund

Opening the Interview

Say it again Confucius!

You can't treat share-holders properly before you treat your workers properly. You cannot know about death until you know about life.

"Two problems opening the interview are getting to a place like a desk where you can present your offerings; and creating immediate interest."

 Creating interest is based around two motivations: positive, the time well spent talking to you & negative, the cost not considering choices.

 Creating awareness of needless loss or risk is achieved by suggesting to your customer there are better cheaper ways to do things.

 The first 2 minutes introducing your presentation are very important. You have 2 minutes to interest him or they could be your last two.

 Sellers must have one rule firmly in mind. You are there to solve problems not to talk about your product. Decision makers want solutions.

 Before you provide a solution, you must find out exactly what his problem is. You must define the problem BEFORE you introduce your product.

"It is always better to sell to a man sitting down. Standing he can walk away from a decision. Sitting it is more difficult for him to escape."

 A customer is more interested talking about himself than listening to you. His issue is as important to him as are his views on the solution.

 Talk as though the business you have to discuss is important to both you & him. Then you'll be half way to him treating it as important too.

 Remember, whatever his business, your customer has something to sell too. So don't be embarrassed selling your product to him.

 A key rule in opening the interview is: make sure you have asked a question beginning HOW/WHY/WHEN/WHERE/WHAT/WHO by the third sentence.

 Using visual aids is vital in selling, particularly intangibles. Seeing is believing. Helps break the line of the desk when you sit together.

 Avoid interruptions in selling. They break concentration. A reasonable courtesy to expect. Interrupted? Re-summarise both back to last point

Say it again Confucius!

A Great Chairman gives approval not for techniques but for the capacity for greater responsibility. A small minded Chairman does the opposite.

Say it again Confucius!

Although you may not wish to use your pet project in sacrifice, the company's bankers would not object to it.

Handling Enquiries

"Smaller companies marketing spend should concentrate on enquiry generation. The key rule is always sell news directed to the relevant name."

 Staff should be trained to handle enquiries enthusiastically. They must be handled while they are still hot & by the seller not his manager.

 The sales manager should NOT pick the fruit of the best enquiries unless he shares the drudgery. This is the reward of planned sales effort.

Questioning for Key Information

"The seller now has to find out is the customer in the market, which product and how should he present it. This means he asks questions."

 The seller's questions follow the pattern of the information he needs to sell his product. They progress from the general to the specific.

 By questioning for this information, the seller assumes the role of advisor. His position is objective. He does not talk about his products.

Say it again Confucius!

A Great Chairman is dignified but not proud. A small minded chairman is proud but not dignified.

HOW TO SELL

Calman

Keynotes for Compelling Sellers
© 2012 Philip R. Lund

Say it again Confucius!

A Great Chairman demands it of himself. A small minded Chairman demands it of others.

A Great Chairman is conscious only of justice; a small minded chairman only of self-interest.

"First he questions to confirm the general company details, size, employees, operations, whatever parameters determine product suitability."

Then he questions specific operational detail so he can place specific product & size; and which of his existing customers are comparators.

Then he ask questions to understand current methods, the problems the customer experiences & the level of operational dissatisfaction.

So at the outset the seller asks questions & hears the story the way the customer tells it. Only when done does he introduce his proposition.

Choice of words is important. Words like sign, order & decision can evoke fear early in the sale but drive towards the decision used later.

So work it out before you say it. From the outset, the best measure of control is to make sure you ask the questions and he does the talking.

Quality of Questions

"Questions provide specific answers, clarify information & establish control. They are either open or leading, direct or indirect."

 Direct questions are used when you know the customer is happy with the purpose of your question: "Who else is quoting for this policy?"

 You use indirect questions to ease the customer's personal attitude to your question: "What are your reasons for asking me to quote?"

 Open questions begin HOW/WHY/WHEN/WHAT/WHO, bring a qualitative response & define the customer attitude to the problem, values & vocabulary.

 Leading questions expecting the answer YES are manipulative, are used to regain control and drive the customer towards a YES decision.

 A customer does 90% of the talking & enjoys the conversation. The seller asks questions, listens & notes. Somewhere lies the key to the sale.

Say it again Confucius!

A great Chairman is accomodating but not one of the crowd. A small minded chairman is one of the crowd but also a source of discord.

Keynotes for Compelling Sellers
© 2012 Philip R. Lund

Say it again Confucius!

A Great Chairman reaches complete understanding of the main issues, a small minded chairman of the minute details.

"Choice of questions depends on the negotiation. Open questions add information or modify direction; leading then open questions reposition it."

 Leading YES/NO questions interrupt the customer flow. A leading YES/NO question followed by an open question introduces a new subject.

 A meeting has only a certain amount of time. It is worth asking how long. Before it ends you must have a clear way forward to the decision.

 The seller must be rigorous in working a tight schedule. Businesslike balance & rhythm to the negotiation gives the best chance of success.

 90% of time the customer is more interested in answering questions than awaiting answers for his own. The 10th time is a question on price.

 A seller must only talk price details after he has talked benefits. People buy value not cost, so they must know what the product does first.

Questioning for Understanding

"It is vital sellers understand what the customer's replies mean. Sales depend on it. Any doubt at all: "What do you mean by that exactly?"

Say it again Confucius!

A Great Chairman cherishes Excellence, a small minded Chairman his own comfort.

 Any doubt as to the customer's real reasoning behind his answers demands clarification: "Why is this issue so important to you?"

 The seller must never assume he understands. He must hear the actual words from the customers mouth. The customer knows what he wants. Ask him.

 The customer's word use will be particular to the customer & his job or business. Listen to them & use them when it is your turn to present.

 Any gap in understanding or piece of information important to the sale which remains unearthed will come back to haunt you at decision time.

 If he fails to answer your question, sits & looks at you, sit & look back. Don't get dragged into answering your own question. He will answer.

Say it again Confucius!

A Great Chairman cherishes rules and regulations, a small minded chairman special favours.

Summarising the Position Reached

"Having gathered information, the seller now summarises to confirm understanding, to emphasise main points & to confirm nothing is omitted."

 Summarising is a key element in selling. It draws a line under the negotiation to confirm full agreement so far & so create a new base point.

 It is also the first time the seller starts talking, recounting the customer's points using the same expression to confirm understanding.

 Again the seller must reconfirm no key point is omitted only to arise as a delay at decision time: "Is there anything else we should include".

Defining the Customer's Issue

"Having gathered information, the seller now summarises to confirm understanding, to emphasise main points & to confirm nothing is omitted."

 Information to hand, the seller now defines the customer's problem. You use only the detail you need without disclosing the cards you hold.

 "From what you have said, can we agree your present system gives you 1..2..3 but you suffer disruptions 1..3..4..and these resulting costs?"

 Obviously the seller weights the advantages and disadvantages of the present system, emphasising values where his product performs strongly.

 The seller must mention the benefits of the present system but show how disadvantages outweigh these values & describe the need for change.

 The trick is to kill with faint praise: "When you bought this system it was clearly the best. Now progress has given us new & better solutions."

 The seller must not exaggerate. He must appear the objective advocate "As you said yourself....." The customer now accepts issues as defined.

Say it again Confucius!

A Great Chairman is easy to serve but hard to please. A small minded chairman is hard to serve but easy to please.

Keynotes for Compelling Sellers
© 2012 Philip R. Lund

The Statement of Intent

"The tempo of the sale increases. Time for the seller's statement of intent. From discussing his problem the customer is now talking business."

 "There seems no good reason to put up with your problems. The alternative we offer gives better service delivery & money back in your bank."

 The seller's credo has nothing to object to. It is assumptive. The words you & your helps the customer visualise the new & better world.

 The seller moves to set a demo or establish a (FTPR) reference. "I should now like to show you how we can provide the solution you seek."

 It's said the salesman never sells, the customer only buys. The way to make him buy is to make the product fit his needs. So what does he need?

Establising the Decision Criteria

"Establishing the criteria for ordering is a technique by which the seller asks the customer to specify his requirements for the new product."

 Properly done, the criteria for ordering what the customer specifies will turn out to be a description of the seller's product.

 Yet again it is essential the seller persuades the customer to list ALL his needs; & he understands exactly what he MEANS by what he says.

 Initially the customer will list 4 or 5 benefits he wants from the change. He expresses himself in benefit terms, what it does not what it is.

 As the customer details these benefits, the seller will be able to ask WHY this choice and HOW it benefits and WHAT about adding these two.

 The seller sifts the reasons carefully. The criteria tell him what the customer wants. The reasons tell him what the customer needs.

 Always remember this. The customer is expert at the problem but you, the seller, are expert at the solution.

Say it again Confucius!

When substance over balances refinement, crudeness results. When refinement overbalances substance, there is superficiality.

Keynotes for Compelling Sellers
© 2012 Philip R. Lund

Say it again Confucius!

When substance and refinement are balanced in one man, you have Excellence.

"Competition, if & when it finally arrives, now has the difficult task of changing the customer's opinion of his needs rather than making it."

 You can now influence the customers decision criteria by adding & prioritising, discounting the relative values of things you do not do so well.

 Success is when the final order & importance of the decision criteria the customer choses describe the benefits the seller's product offers.

 Every decision we make involves some level of compromise. Nothing ever gives you everything you want and, if it does, it costs too much.

 The reasons we buy are strictly personal. One man buys a car for comfort another for speed. We are all customers & customers are people too

 Then we find the new product we bought changes our view of what products in this area should deliver & having decided, our priorities change.

 These things are just a fact of life. We have to satisfy requirements while we live & accept one decision will ultimately replace another.

 While determining & structuring the customer's ordering criteria, the seller will add values like "Well that's worth doing straight away."

"When you install our system, your staff will have none of these problems. Instead........" Assumption is basic to the art of selling.

 And the seller will be assumptive. He will assume the customer will buy. He helps visualise the new product installed and in operation

 MY OUR YOU YOUR following WHEN are all key words used by the seller who sells assumptively. This is a joint decision.

Say it again Confucius!

How pleasant it is to repeat what we are learning. How happy we are when a friend returns from a long trip.

Keynotes for Compelling Sellers
© 2012 Philip R. Lund

Say it again Confucius!

In his actions he avoids violence & disrespect. In his appearance he seeks sincerity. In his speech he avoids vileness & vulgarity.

...and Summarise

"The summary of the criteria for ordering draws a line under this step in the sale. It confirms questioning in this area is complete."

 "May I confirm these are the criteria you are seeking to satisfy with your decision. First you said....was of utmost importance..Second.."

 "Are there any other factors we have omitted?" The customer brings forward any other criteria. The seller weighs & positions them in his list.

 The customer will say if he feels he is misstated. The line drawn by agreement at this point must be argument proof; or the sale will escape.

The Trial Close

Crunch time. The second most important question in selling "If I could...., would you....?" The trial close. "If I could...., would you....?"

 "You specified a product to do this & that with blue there & bells & whistles here. If I could supply this, would you place the order today?"

 Difficult to refuse. The customer has agreed this is what he wants. You have repeated him in his words & asked. "If I could.., would you..?"

 If not, WHY not? You need to know WHY the trial close is not accepted & sort it out now. If you can't, the sale is not worth continuing.

 The one proviso is cost. Be good to add. "If I could...AND show you a profit/lower cost on current methods, would you give me your order now?"

 From now on, the trial close (If I could..., would you...?) is used throughout the sale to establish/confirm agreement & maintain commitment.

Say it again Confucius!

A racehorse is not praised for its might but for its thorough-bred qualities.

Keynotes for Compelling Sellers
© 2012 Philip R. Lund

Prehandling Objections

"Objections are to be welcomed in the sale. They tell you the state of customer thinking. Some are sincere (fact), some insincere (emotional)."

 Sincere objections must be answered, insincere objections challenged. Objections you know you will face must be prehandled to limit impact.

 Objections to prehandle are usually based on hesitancy to decide, his case is special, competition, hearsay; & changing circumstances.

 Prehandling makes objections easy to agree early in the sale when less depends. Price queries can only be handled after value is shown.

 "Worth having these savings (doing) now, isn't it? Company X use it & now can't live without it. Everyone can't be wrong." This won't change.

Say it again Confucius!

Not to alter one's faults is to be faulty indeed.

Keynotes for Compelling Sellers
© 2012 Philip R. Lund

Handling Competition

"Sellers face 3 types of competition: customers doing nothing, buying something entirely different, or buying a directly competitive product."

 3 rules in handling competition are know everything there is to know about them, never ever mention them by name; & never knock them.

 Knowing competition, you know the can & the can't do, mentioning by name is free advertising; & knocking them knocks you. Try faint praise!

 Fear of changing to something that won't work out, a natural disinclination to spend & reduced choices create hesitancy in decision making

 Seller's questions "What do you have in mind" preempts "Its not what I had in mind" as "When will you want it" preempts "I won't need it yet."

 Sellers must follow gut feeling & clear out now any objection which will cause decision hesitancy if he's to close the sale across the table.

Say it again Confucius!

I was not born knowing what I teach you. Being fond of the past, I sought it through diligence.

Say it again Confucius!

Be a great man among scholars! Don't be a small minded man!

Natural decision inertia must be overcome early too. "From the values that will flow from your decision, isn't this is a must do now?"

 Hearsay objections are inevitable when you have established markets. Third party referees will confirm the competitor is only trouble making.

 Price will raise its head time & again. Explain & minimise "20p per day but let me be more specific when I know your precise specifications."

 Customers know changes mean new issues. The trick is to be assumptive. Identify the problem then show it really isn't a problem in practice.

Emails v Letters

"Emails in selling are fast communication. But while letters can sit in judgement on you or the decision maker, emails can easily be trashed."

 Letters or emails should be answered promptly. But maybe they should be answered by telephone & the opportunity taken to set the meeting.

 Be careful too. Letters in sales can sit around to condemn you later while, with emails, you could be writing to a wider circulated audience.

 Make sure you stay close to the truth. Never lie on paper. Never criticise staff or competition. They WILL return to haunt you.

 In sales, if there is any doubt, don't say it. Whatever you do, don't write it. The battle you want to win is the order, not the argument.

Say it again Confucius!

When the weather turns cold, we realise that the pines and firs are the last to fade.

Say it again Confucius!

When 3 of us are walking together I am sure I have a teacher. His competencies I imitate, his incompetencies I avoid.

...and Quotations

"In sales, quotations not properly handled are a danger area too. In sales management terms, number & value of quotes is a very risky measure."

 The one great rule with quotes is try to avoid writing them. Once you give the customer the information he doesn't need to talk to you again.

 If the customer likes the seller but wants him out without causing upset, what should he do? Ask for a quotation and the seller leaves happy.

 Quotes again diminish competitive advantage. The one most comparable thing with them is the price, a poor medium to show benefit value.

 So why does the customer need quotes when you are there to tell him the answers. Board meetings? Then only quote when he confirms he will buy.

 If your customer 'may want' your product next year, give him your quote next year when price is probably higher. Don't waste time this year.

 No-one has the right to waste your time. If the customer wants your quote, you should demand his decision timetable on his intended YES.

Keynotes for Compelling Sellers
© 2012 Philip R. Lund

"Where quotes are the norm, it is a good idea to carry a document which you can complete as a quote & push across the table for signature."

 How do you eat an elephant? Small pieces? Where the price is high or the project long, better to quote separately priced interrelated phases.

 Formal quotes should be brief, in a form likely to be read. And keep the lawyers away. Complicated conditions should follow a signed intent.

 If the quote is for one man, deliver it by hand & sign him up. For Boards, why not make that presentation yourself & handle any objections.

 So the rule. Avoid quotes. If you must, make sure it only confirms agreements made. Then it may convert to an order & with a decision path!

 We understand what the customer wants & how. We checked understanding is mutual, prehandled objections & put competition to bed. Now to sell!

Say it again Confucius!

A hamlet of 10 homes will surely contain someone as loyal & reliable as me but none will equal my love of learning.

Sell Benefits

"Unless he's buying a Monet or a Ferrari, customers buy a product for its benefits: your machine for what it does, your policy for its cover."

 Benefits are what customers gain from using your product. He's told things he wants to gain. You have to show how your product delivers them.

 Your product has characteristics delivering advantages or benefits. His words described benefits, not characteristics. Sellers show the link.

 If you describe your product, the customer won't twig how it delivers what he wants. Sellers match his words to describe product & function.

"Unless selling to a technican, don't talk technical. He won't understand it. NO UNDER-STANDING, NO SALE. HOW it does it, not WHAT it does."

 The customer lists what he wants. The seller shows how the product features deliver it. And he shows the other benefits that come with it.

 So the seller innovates on the customer's need. "You not only get this you want but you get this & that which gives you that & this for free".

 Before you go out and sell, make a list of ALL your product features. List ALL related benefits against each. Learn them. You'll need them...

 ...and different industries use same products in different ways, lawyers for deeds, accountants for accounts. Policies cover mortgages & wives.

Say it again Confucius!

I dislike the way clever talkers disrupt companies & homes, purple encroaches on red & modern tunes play riot with elegant music.

Keynotes for Compelling Sellers
© 2012 Philip R. Lund

Let the Benefits Flow

The words 'which means' link features to benefits. So it goes "...which means...which means.. not only that" and you have a benefit chain.

 A 3 litre car is fast which means you overtake quickly which means you're safer. Not only that, you'll be less tired with the wife just as wanted!

 Negative benefit chains show what will be missing. 1.5 litre is slow, takes for ever to get there, exhausted when you get home. Who wants that?

 Every order criterion should relate to a feature with a benefit flow which cover the criterion. Each time the buyer confirms, point covered.

...and Summarise again

"The customer has listed what he wants (1/2/3). He has agreed the product delivers these needs (1/2/3) "Are you now happy to place your order?"

 Well planned the customer can only say YES. Each reason to buy is agreed as is the product feature to deliver it. YES? "How much is it first."

 Again use words YOU & YOUR in benefit selling. Paint word pictures to help the customer image the product or service in use in his operation.

 Empahasise value whenever possible to reduce the impact of the price announcement & to increase the urgency of a YES decision.

Say it again Confucius!

Remain sincere in purpose while studying widely. Continue to think while posing frank & open questions.

Say it again Confucius!

If an urn lacks the characteristics of an urn, how can we call it an urn?

"Be enthusiastic. If you're not, noone else will be. Don't exaggerate claims. Enthusiasm increases credibility, exaggeration decreases it."

 Technical evidence should only prove related benefits. Once technical discussion goes beyond this, chances are the sale is moving off course.

 Don't get caught in the trap of talking most strongly about the things you do least well & so making this quite clear to the customer.

 Having agreed your product benefits give the customer all he wants, time to ask for the order. Extra talking risks saying the wrong things.

 Keep your talking to a minimum, enough to prove the point. Remember. You're there to solve his problems not to boast about your successes.

Demos

"The customer will now either ask for a demo or a quote, make a sincere or insincere objection, prefer a competitor, ask how much or say YES."

Say it again Confucius!

Do not be swayed by personal opinion, recognise no inescapable necessity, do not be stubborn, do not be self-centred.

 All products must be demo'ed so sell by visual aids, presentations or site visits. The more difficult to demo, the more important the demo.

 Service products can be difficult to demo; but eg death notices in the newspaper list every day people who did not think they would die.

 "If a picture paints 1000 words.." Demos prove product benefits. One-to-one they are highly emotive & increase the customer desire to own.

 Selling equipment, the rule is: sell the magic of the machine. Don't distract by talking too much. Use a script to cover important points.

 Before beginning agree the objectives of the demo."If you like what you see, are you going to buy one?" Sets the tone, concentrates the mind.

 Once the demo objectives are achieved, end it. There is nothing left to demo. Don't be tempted to demo the impossible. Ask him for his order.

Keynotes for Compelling Sellers
© 2012 Philip R. Lund

Say it again Confucius!

In our natures we approximate one another, habits put us further apart. The only ones who do not change are wise men & idiots.

"If you demo or present to a group, take a colleague. Then you can separate the decision maker from the art critics & focus on his requirements."

 Don't misuse the demo & make the product do more than intended. It can help the sale but it can lose it. Tight demos mean high interest.

 Beware leaving products on free trial. Free means no commitment & you're selling commitment. It also suggests no value. You're selling value.

 If the customer is in a hurry for your product but wants to see it first, why not take the order provisional on him being happy with the demo.

 Exhibitions tend to introduce products & skim the most interested. For smaller companies the money is better spent on quality direct contact.

...and Visual Aids

"Visual aids are essential in selling because they present sales messages thru the eyes and ears, building on meaning & interest."

 The reason why sellers do not use visual aids is they take time to prepare. Preparing visual aids is an important matter of sales discipline.

 Visual aids are made to match the sales presentation from before & after photos, letters from satisfied customers to something good to hold.

 Products you have something to demo. A service is intangible so how to make it visual? Cleanliness is a concept. You can show something clean.

 Never use brochures as visual aids. The customer is likely to tell you he has seen enough, leave the brochure & he will call if interested.

 Owners often like a film show of their company but they are expensive, usually out of date & risk turning the customer into an art critic.

 Seat the customer to present visual aids. Sit alongside & break the desk line. Presenting to a group, be sure they are all on the same page.

 Selling professional services the presentation needs to hit your target service gap. Then it is a matter of approach, methodology & gravitas

Say it again Confucius!

A gentleman who prefers his own ease is no gentleman.

Keynotes for Compelling Sellers
© 2012 Philip R. Lund

...and PowerPoint

Say it again Confucius!

Then upright friend, the devoted & the learned friend benefit us. The fawning friend, the flattering and the too eloquent harm us.

"PowerPoint slides are ideal to cover who we are, what we do & how, our principles, benefits that flow, who we did it for & a case study."

 Sales presentations answer the questions "Does he want it?" & "Does he want it from you?" And set up the conversation "How can he have it?"

 The way you present should be vivid & exciting, forcible and friendly. Before presenting with colleagues make sure first who is in command.

 If a seller of high value services thinks he can rely on his golden voice & his gaze alone, he should visit a psychiatrist or job counsellor.

Use References

"No sale is over when the order is taken. Your job is to ensure he is happy with its use. Happy customers make strong third party references."

 It is far easier to sell when you can reference a list of happy customers. You can make a demo succeed but customers prove products in use.

 So good sellers do not neglect existing customers. His word can replace a demo. A call to him can help take an order over the table.

 No product is perfect in use. But the judgement will be based on how you, the seller, respond to his issues. Make sure he has your number.

Say it again Confucius!

To become rich and honoured through injustices, for me such joy may be compared to an evanescent cloud.

Say it again Confucius!

To eat vegetables without meat, to drink only water, to have only one's bent arm as a pillow, there can be joy in such a life.

"A warning. Say nothing about a customer except things you would not mind him hearing. It's a good motto in life too. Bad news travels fast!"

 Thru the sale the customer asks questions, gives opinions. The seller answers questions, modifies opinions & confirms understanding/agreement.

 The seller has established ordering criteria & shows how product benefits deliver them. Moving to decision, customer questions become citical

 Customer objections identify questions he must satisfy to say YES. Is he pointing direction or just vacillating to delay making a decision?

Trial Close Again

Trial closes determine whether objections are sincere or insincere. "If I could satisfy this point, would you be happy to place your order?"

 If the customer responds YES to the trial close, the seller now answers the point, agrees & closes for the order. "Are happy now to proceed?"

 If the customer answers the trial close with another objection, then his objections are insincere. Maybe there's a gap in your presentation.

Say it again Confucius!

A Great Chairman's doctrine consists solely of loyalty and reciprocrity.

Say it again Confucius!

A Chairman's term of office depends on his uprightness. He who goes on living without it escapes disaster only by good fortune.

Handling Sincere Objections

You have to battle with a sincere objection to take his order. If it goes on, you get to "I am here to talk business. What's the real issue?."

 With sincere objections, the question "why is that a particular problem for you?" identifies the road to a satisfying answer & the way ahead.

 Sincere objections should be welcomed – a real desire for clarity; a way to clear the head to reach the decision. Certainly beats silence!

 Many objections at the stage of the sale relate to an emotional hesitancy to make a decision in a 'better the devil you know' kind of way.

 The seller overcomes fear of decision risk by refering to happy users, good closing to ease the decision & stressing any guarantee aspects.

 He overcomes inconvenience of change or present satisfaction emphasising the high value & savings from change & renewed operator happiness.

"To avoid a decision a customer may raise small doubts which hardly require answer. Wait till he wants an answer, close firmly, remain silent."

 He overcomes fear of colleague criticism by making sure the customer has the numbers & counter aruments he needs to define new benefit flow.

 He overcomes new cost by showing higher new value, the 'no brainer' arguments for a decision 'not worth not taking' immediately.

 Particularly he overcomes delaying the decision by showing the real value of a decision now. Let's face it. One less problem to worry about.

 Silence is a tool sellers use to 'pressure' the customer to reach his decision. Don't respond to his pressure by answering your own question.

 Don't be drawn into a sparring match with a customer even when you're right. The first heavy blow you land will knock the order out the door.

 A facetious objection can be killed off by turning it back as a question "Why are you happier with dirty vehicles than clean vehicles?"

 If you hit prejudice or emotional attitudes, you must go back to agreements already reached & ask WHY this should be a particular issue.

Say it again Confucius!

If a man is sparing in his reproaches of others while he heaps them upon himself, he will certainly keep away resentments.

Keynotes for Compelling Sellers
© 2012 Philip R. Lund

Say it again Confucius!

I have seen & heard of men who, upon finding competence strove with might & main to equal it. I have yet however to meet such men.

"And don't be persuaded to chase after rabbits he sends running for you. He will see you as a fool & that is a real reason not to do business."

Objections can come anytime in the sale & you can choose when to answer them – now if it adds, later when it fits or never if better avoided.

An objection based on a weak argument can be reduced to its logical absurdity but be careful not to be seen to mock your 'bread maker.'

Reasoned objections can be out-weighed by far greater advantages, overcome by showing it not an issue or weakened as not an issue in practice.

As you know your product disadvantages so you should know the solutions Every product has both. Present your case & let the customer chose.

"If your product doesn't suit customer needs, bow out and gain that respect. It is ethical selling & you won't store problems into the future."

 But be sure you understand correctly "Am I right to say this is the issue?" Seeing the target clearly gives the best chance of hitting it.

 The meeting where you hit the final objection is when you should take the order. Customer desire is highest. He wants to make a decision.

 So don't get caught leaving the room to find the objection answer. You'll lose decision momentum. Take the order subject to satisfaction.

 Objections move naturally to a close "I'd have it if it's blue not red." (Why blue?) "If I provide a blue one, will you place your order now?"

Say it again Confucius!

To the Sales Director: 'Require of others only what you have first taught them'. Asked for additional guidance: 'Never grow weary'.

Selling Against Competition

"The rule in selling against competition is to set the criteria for ordering with the customer which competitors cannot satisfy."

 It's the same with success in tender selling. Make sure you are there when the specification is prepared so to suit your product.

 You don't bring up competitors but they may appear. The trick is to congratulate heartily the things they do but the customer doesn't want.

 Sometimes the competitor does have the better product to suit needs. Why not suggest the customer asks to add other aspects to his order foc.

 Rules v competition – Don't knock/ mention by name. Use their weakness to highlight your benefits, emphasise ones hopelessly out of the race.

 At the end of the day, the difference between two similar products is the difference between the two people selling them – a matter of pride.

 If your customer is leaning towards competition, treat it as an insult to your own ability & kick your backside for not getting there sooner.

Price is an Objection

"So how much is all this going to cost me?" You have reached the price objection & it must be carefully handled, a hurdle you have to jump.

 Price can only be an objection. It can never be a seling benefit. No-one buys things because they're cheap. They must want them first.

 Price must always be described in its most glamorous form. Daily/weekly costs look better than annual. $1 per day looks better than $365pa.

 Similarly savings look better in their greatest form, annual rather than weekly. Make sure you have the numbers right or death is certain.

 Relate costs to the familiar – "Less than a pint of beer". Use pen & paper to show cost in its simplest form with options shown as optional.

 Going for Board decision be sure your customer knows numbers & arguments. Put numbers to intangibles such as better service & machine uptime.

 If your product is more expensive than a competitor's, you have to show additional value. People buy what they see as best value for money.

Say it again Confucius!

Don't worry about holding high position but rather about playing a proper role. Nor that no one knows you. Seek to be worth knowing.

Say it again Confucius!

I can do nothing about cases of satisfaction without self-reflection or of compliance without self-reformation.

"A high priced product may seem less expensive compared to one of even higher price. Cost less savings may show higher price as a lower price."

 Cost of product in process manufacturing depends on throughput, wastage & service outcomes. Lower prices in retail may mean lower margins.

 If you accept $100 means less to a rich than a poor man, then $1000 has lower value to a company than a person. Company money is being spent.

 If you think your product is expensive, your customer will pick this up. Decide on what makes it inexpensive before your first call; or fail.

 The more the relative expense of your product, the closer you must stay to your presentation. Let the customer decide on your best case.

 Don't break price under pressure. You'll lose credibility. If you must give 'a taste of something', do it in payment terms or free delivery.

 The more important you make your product seem to the customer, the less important price will be & the less likely price will be an objection.

 Price is the last objection, your task to show price as good value for the benefits. Satisfy the value question & you have yourself an order/

Making the Decision

"In any sale a customer must make 3 decisions. Does he want it? Does he want it from you? How can he have it? The 3rd decision is equally key."

 Decisions to act will relate to things like finance arrangements, trade-ins or Group strategy. Inventive proposals must find the clear way.

 If your customer wants your product, then he must have it. The seller's job is to put forward proposals until he finds the one he can act on.

 If you keep banging on with "Are you ready to act now?" You will lose good customers & maybe good friends. 3 times & find a better proposal!

 We have summarised & agreed with the customer his ordering criteria, the benefit delivery of his needs at good value. Let's close this sale.

Say it again Confucius!

There may be some who create things without knowledge; but I am not of that type.

After being taught much, I selected the best and followed it. I observed much and remembered it.

Closing the Sale

"The shortest route is the best route to an order. If you do not close across the table first call, you'll have to go back for a second call."

 First rule for the second call is always make the appointment before you leave the first call. It removes the risk of the customer delaying.

 The second rule is only call back when you have something new to ask or offer. Shooting the breeze is not a call objective.

 If you have made your customer a market for your product, make sure you follow-up quickly or you will have set the table for your competitor.

"Second calls after a demo should produce orders. What else is there to talk about? Stick to the timetable, retrace to your agreements – CLOSE!"

 Only call back to the customer's premises when you have a physical reason to be there ie a site check, a quote, a contract. Time is valuable.

 Closing for order leads to objections & signatures & should be handled face-to-face. If the customer wants you there, make sure you know WHY.

 Don't give professional advice on subjects you're not equipped to handle; & don't make a meal of site surveys. You sell. Installers install.

 If you must bring a 'specialist', make sure he understands pre-call he only answers your questions. Technicians prefer the detail to the sale.

Say it again Confucius!

If you are humble, you will not be laughed at. If you are magnanimous, you will attract many to your side.

Keynotes for Compelling Sellers
© 2012 Philip R. Lund

Say it again Confucius!

If you are sincere, people will trust you; diligent, you will be successful; & gracious, you will get on well with subordinates.

Know When to Close

"The basic rules are: Keep the sale simple, take the order as soon as you can; & only one of you should be doing the selling – YOU."

 Knowing when to close is about listening for the customers buying signals: "How quickly can you deliver?" "What are the payment terms?" etc.

 Answering the buying signal followed by "Would you like to go ahead on this basis?" is the close; but do not lose your way in the excitement.

 Never be afraid to ask for the decision. You can't lose what you haven't got! But keep hold of the ability to return to where you left off.

 When selling,be the optimist. Keep this thought in your mind – I am bound to be successful. It is only a question of when.

 The ABC of selling – ALWAYS BE CLOSING.

Know How to Close

"Rule 1 in knowing how to close is to ask for the order and THEN BE SILENT. Silence puts pressure on the customer to make a decision."

 Decisions to spend money are difficult. The customer needs your help. If you start talking, you break his concentration. Sit there in silence.

 You will never talk a customer to exhaustion & his order. It is easier to talk yourself out of a good decision than talk yourself into it.

 In making his decision, the customer may talk. Be silent. If he ask a question, answer simply & be silent. If he is silent, close again.

 The second rule in knowing how to close is to make the decision easy for the customer. Most closing techniques avoid the direct question.

 Offering trial quantities can be the best way for a commodity salesman to break the grip of a single supplier; but deliver excellent quality.

Say it again Confucius!

Rotten wood may not be carved, nor a wall of manure or dirt plastered.

Keynotes for Compelling Sellers
© 2012 Philip R. Lund

Say it again Confucius!

Juniors are to be respected! How do we know they will not be our equals in the future?

"Remember in selling for every disadvantage there is an advantage. It is just that sometimes the advantage is a little more difficult to find."

 Sell interdependent products as a package, not one by one. Same with retail. Put together the package he wants for one decision & signature.

 Sell independent products one by one. Once he starts signing he will sign again so take the second order provisional on success of the first.

 With the choice to sell high or low, sell high. More normally costs more & maybe is the better customer choice. You can always agree low.

6 Closing Techniques

"Here we mention 6 closing techniques: the direct, the assumptive, the alternative, the step-by-step, the supposition & the provisional order."

 Only the direct close asks the question directly: Would you like to go ahead?/ place your order? The rest assume the decision is already made.

 The Assumptive Close assumes it is only a matter of HOW/WHEN/WHERE – How do you like to pay? When do you want it? Where shall we install it?

 The Alternative Close assume it is only a choice of alternatives – a blue one or a red one?, a large or a small one?, Wednesday or Thursday?

 The Step-by-step Close uses a sequence of YES's to close on a YES. Ideal in commodity/retail selling: 6 blue? YES, 3 red? YES, sign here? YES.

 The Supposition Close says "Suppose I did this & that, put that there & added a blue one, could we go ahead on that basis?" Trial close format.

 The Provisional Order Close takes the order despite things beyond your control: "To speed delivery let's place the order subject to Board."

Keynotes for Compelling Sellers
© 2012 Philip R. Lund

Say it again Confucius!

At home be humble; at work respectful; with others be loyal. Even among foreigners you may not abandon these precepts.

Contracts

"The seller should always carry a contract to sign, even with waivers, while the emotional levels are high. The decision is likely to stick."

 The more complicated the contract the more important it is to have a 'buy now agree details later' clause before the lawyers become involved.

 Clever legal jargon refering to unknown Acts creates doubt and prejudices sales. Terms covering how the agreement will play out are more useful.

 After signature, thank him and congratulate his decision. Answer further queries, give your contact details & put the contract in your pocket.

After the Sale

"The sale does not end with the order. Selling is rendering a service whereby the customer gets what he ordered & at the time he expects it."

 The customer will feel some doubt at the time the product is delivered. The seller's task is to make sure the first impression are good ones.

 You can only make promises you know you can keep; but, just as you fought for your order, so you fight for your customer to deliver service.

Say it again Confucius!

Wisdom has no doubts. Good management has no concerns. Courage is without fear.

Say it again Confucius!

You think I am hiding things from you. I have no secrets. I do nothing I do not share with you. I'm that kind of person.

...and Manage the Customer

"Post delivery, make sure the signatory is happy; but staff cooperation is key to operational success. You must resell the benefits to both."

 If you sold high in the company, you must resell to the department manager otherwise he may kill it to prove to his boss he knows better.

 You must keep contact with your decision maker.If there are multi-level responsibilities create a multilevel team to manage the relationship.

 At worst, your customer is a favourable 3rd party reference, at best he will reorder. So make sure you treat him well.

 Resell the benefits of your relationship regularly to keep competitors at bay. Handle issues promptly even those of small consequence.

 Treat product objections as you treated objections in the sale, personally and face-toface. Make sure the customer knows where to find you.

 If something goes wrong with delivery or installation, don't delegate. The customer wants solutions. Take over the problem & get him solutions.

"Don't be persuaded to join your customer in talking your company down. Once he hears your dismal stories he will know all is lost."

 Remember too that all equipment can break down & still perform its promised task. Emphasise service benefits that deliver promised outputs.

 If the customer wants to bawl you out, let him. No principles are involved. Do not disagree. Sit quietly &, when he has finished, continue.

 If the customer continues to be unhappy tell him his issues are capable of solution too. Then take over the problem & get him solutions.

 The customer could just be plain angry. Tell him he is wrong to be angry & you'll lose the war. Keep quiet; let the tirade pass. Keep WHY? in mind.

 Finally, be over-familiar with your product but never your customer. Always treat him with respect. Then you can never go wrong.

Say it again Confucius!

With the portion of management that's above average one may speak of higher things; with those below it one may not.

Keynotes for Compelling Sellers
© 2012 Philip R. Lund

Say it again Confucius!

We must always be adaptable. When the ford water is deep, I use stepping stones. When it is shallow, I take off my shoes & socks.

The Sale: A Summary

"Now let's summarise. These are the rules of selling or any form of persuasion. Tuck them away. Practice them until they become second nature."

 There is only one way to sell & that is through face-to-face contact. Only when in front of your customer can you take his initial order.

 No-one sells sitting in his office or at home. To deliver your target sales you must meet the planned number & spread of customers each week.

 Plan your market & sales objectives. Initiate control procedures to make sure you work your plan. Use a little mind and be effective.

 The lucky seller is the busy seller. Cover ground. Kick up as much dust as you can. You never know where the next surprise order is coming from.

 The customer knows you are there to sell him so don't be embarrassed. He wants to be sold by a professional and to make the right decision.

 Selling & buying are part of the business game. The rules are agreed between the players. Your advantage is to set the rules from the outset.

"You know the questions you will ask to suit your presentation. The customer must wait to see your move. He answers the questions you choose."

 The customer will undertake early commitment "If we can do this better & cheaper than you can now, will you consider a change?" WHY NOT?

 Words are important in selling. It is not only what you say but how you say it. Two words out of order can break the spell & the sale is lost.

 At the call, don't let your own brilliance overcome you. Talk straight, talk sense & talk business, the single objective to take the order.

 Go to every call properly prepared. Seek the information from your questions that construct your argument, from the general to the specific.

 At every meeting it should be your objective to take the order. AIM HIGH. You can always settle for a secondary objective, say a presentation.

 A seller is never better than at the first meeting. Customer interest is high. Interest can be turned into desire for your product; & closed.

 Customers react positively to good vigorous selling. If you buy something you like to be sold & convinced. Give that pleasure to the customer.

Say it again Confucius!

A great Chairman is sparing in his words but prodigal in deeds. He seeks to be slow of speech but quick of action.

Keynotes for Compelling Sellers
© 2012 Philip R. Lund

Say it again Confucius!

Good management is no remote ideal! We only have to desire it and straightaway it arrives.

"The reasons to buy are logical but the decision to make a decision is emotional. A good seller can make it come, recognise it & close it."

 The decision to buy is heard as a 'buying signal'. "How long does it take to install?" Stop what you are doing, answer the question; & close.

 How many calls to order? If you organise to close each meeting, you'll take the shortest, safest route. Too long & you'll become boring.

 Whatever the customer says, you must understand the WHAT & the WHY he is saying. Somewhere in his statements lies the seed to sale's success.

 The seller is the expert in the market under discussion. As technology has moved on, his product will innovate on the customer's opportunity.

 The customer is expert on his issues. The seller must ask questions to understand the real problem & explain the dimensions of his solution.

 You must sell to decision makers. If your contact says he must confirm any decision with another man, he's the one you should be talking to.

 No amount of selling will sell to the wrong man. Try to reset with both of them; or start again. Your time is better spent elsewhere.

Opening statements must be high impact. "I've got something here that is really going to interest you." "Really. What is that?" Off you go.

 You want your customer to respect you as professional. It is easier to say NO to a friend than an expert when the evidence is against you.

 Speak well of competition if not by name. Otherwise you'll wear an albatross around your neck. Customers know you think your product better.

 Talk about him. Ask him questions. People love to talk about themselves & the decisions they make. You are 2 people about to settle a problem.

 Expressing random opinions can destroy. They don't sell. Stay uncommitted. Information that cannot be used for you can be used against you.

 HOW WHY WHEN WHERE WHAT WHO questions tell you what & why the customer wants to buy. Questions expecting YES/NO take back control & redirect.

 Questions moving from general to specific tell you about his business & the problems you are there to solve. Listen to the words he uses.

 Guide & control him thru every aspect of his needs. Mould & weight his answers so he describes his problem in terms of your product offering.

Say it again Confucius!

He whose language is unrestrained will have difficulty doing it all.

Keynotes for Compelling Sellers
© 2012 Philip R. Lund

Say it again Confucius!

A Great Chairman's attitude is such that he shows no preferences; but he is prejudiced in favour of justice.

"Summarise with him his statement of his problem, the things he needs. Agree there are no other factors & the importance of an early decision."

 Introduce your product/service using his words. You need to show capability to deliver. Keep technical detail to an understandable minimum.

 Use visual aids. Slides, pictures, products, graphs exist & add visual to mental understanding, giving life to intangible/service concepts.

 Paint word pictures. Imagine using the product, its trouble free simplicity, its purpose-built suitability. Walk around. Gain/hold attention.

 If you talk nothing else, talk benefits. If you state a quality "It is fast" state the benefit "It will save you time & money in operation."

 Develop the benefit chain "which means you have clean trucks" & the negative chain "rather than dirty trucks hanging around the streets."

 Ask him what each benefit means to him. Make him commit to important benefits. These factors will influence his emotional decision to buy.

 Query & destroy any points you think are irrelevant or dangerous. Add one or two benefits you know weigh heavily in favour of your product.

Turn his statements back as direct questions for agreement "Do you agree this factor is particularly important in any decision you make?" YES.

 Summarise & agree each of the factors basic to the sale. These are criteria you agreed through questioning which will determine his decision.

 Personalise what you say with the words YOU and YOUR. It is what it will do for YOU It is the great advantages it will bring YOUR company.

 Couple YOU & YOUR with the assumption he already has the product: "With YOUR system installed & operational, YOU will no longer have......

 Talk advantages, not disadvantages. He will soon pick these out unless you prehandle them by building the opposite case in your presentation.

 The only disadvantages you mention are the ones that turn out to be advantages. It draws him to you for your honesty & reflects real values.

 If he picks a real disadvantage you must provide the answer.Perhaps it won't affect him or is a small price to pay for other real advantages.

 Control the conversation. Avoid interruptions "May I come back to this later?" Control the ball: make him play it to you as you play it to him.

Say it again Confucius!

A Great Chairman, out of pride, does not engage in strife; out of consideration for the whole group he does not join cliques.

Say it again Confucius!

If one is sedate in the presence of work-people, they will be respectful. If one is considerate and kind, they will be loyal.

"Compare new & existing situations. Commit to answers. Is this better for you? YES. And this? YES. This? YES. Would you like to go ahead? YES."

 Resummarise the benefits that deliver what he told you he wants. Agree them. These are the arguments for your product. Force them home.

 YES becomes the easiest answer. You have given him the logic for a decision & created the emotional envirnoment in which he can decide.

 Chose your close. The direct, strong close for a YES/NO answer ie Would you like to place your order on this basis to achieve delivery March?

 Or do you assume he will place his order? It is just a matter WHEN would he like delivery? WHERE to installed it? Or HOW to pay for it?

 Maybe you assume he will buy. It's a matter of choice. Would he like a red one or a blue one? Or would he like the big one or the small one?

 If the customer continues with a series of insincere objections, you must challenge "Why you are not happy to do business on this basis?"

"If the answer to the CLOSE is "NO," maybe you have missed key information in your questioning. Go back to your last point of agreement."

 But maybe it's some small problem you can easily overcome or outweigh with benefits when you know the real reason "Can you tell me why not?"

 Logically the customer will buy except for the reasons why not. Understand these reasons, provide the solutions & you have yourself a sale.

 The most important word in selling after YES is WHY. If you get a NO ask WHY & continue to ask WHY until you get the answer vital to the sale.

 If you believe your product is expensive in relation to the benefits it delivers, your customer will too. Get your head clear on this one.

 Also to close successfully you must believe there is no good reason for your customer not to order straight away. Any doubt you will pass on.

 Finally, do not oversell. You can easily lose an order by making exaggerated claims you cannot meet. A fool and his customer are soon parted

Say it again Confucius!

Be not concerned over men not knowing you. Be concerned rather over your own failings.

Keynotes for Compelling Sellers
© 2012 Philip R. Lund

Say it again Confucius!

To feel no resentment though poor is difficult; not to be proud though rich is easy.

Keynotes for Compelling Sellers
© 2012 Philip R. Lund

"Do not undersell. Aim high, settle lower if you must. You cannot lose an order you haven't got; but you will lose it if you do not ask for it."

 And finally, again! REMEMBER THIS if nothing else. NO is never an acceptable answer in selling if the customer needs your product.

 Selling is like catching a mouse without a trap. Lunge, he escapes. Continually reduce the room left to move in & he will hop into your hand.

Epilogue

"Sales books tend to be for newcomers or stories from the trenches. What about the professional who comes back looking for new inspiration?."

 Sales training is about blinding flashes of the obvious. Learning is about trying & succeeding so you go forward & don't revert to old ways.

 Top salesmen cut down their presentations to reduce sales time per order. They need something "Compelling" to refeed & rebalance quality.

 Sellers need to know how to handle objections, sell benefits etc. but real learning come from selling in tandem ie do it this way, not that.

 Key to knowing how to sell is understanding the framework of a sale, the sequence of interrelated steps that lead from 1st contact to order.

 The sales framework answers the 3 key questions in any sale: Does he want it? Does he want it from you? How is he going to have it?

 Does he want it? learning covers asking open questions, establishing ordering criteria, prehandling objections & agreeing the point reached.

Say it again Confucius!

A Great Chairman follows a three lane highway: good management, wisdom and courage.
"The Chairman is his own highway".

Keynotes for Compelling Sellers
© 2012 Philip R. Lund

Say it again Confucius!

The end has indeed arrived! I have yet to meet a man as fond of excellence as he is of outward appearances.

"Does he want it from you? learning relates benefit flows to ordering criteria, knocks out competitors & agrees benefits match & deliver needs."

 How is he going to have it? learning covers handling final objections, putting together tempting offers, closing & keeping the customer sold.

 "It's too easy to be unstructured and believe, if the prospect likes you, you are going to take the order." Quote from a Seller.

 "Without a well structured approach to selling you end up in a lot of pleasant conversations going nowhere." Quote from a Seller.

 Great sellers have the singular ability to want to kick themselves round the block each time they mess up a sale. It's the best way to learn.

 I suppose, if you think selling is an inherent ability, it boils down to whose mother was best at giving it voice.

 Where, outside selling, do you get a NO, say "If I do this & this and get you this & that, will you say YES?" "YES."

Keynotes for Compelling Sellers
© 2012 Philip R. Lund